Socialism:

It's a Dog's Life

Socialism: It's a Dog's Life

David L. Cates

Cherry Creek Press
New Mexico

Copyright @ 2020 by David L. Cates

All rights reserved. No part of this book may be reproduced in any form or by any electronic or mechanical means, including information storage and retrieval systems, without permission in writing from the publisher.

ISBN 978-1-7339849-0-4

Some characters and events in this book are fictitious. Any similarity to real persons, living or dead, is coincidental and not intended by the author.

Illustrator: Clara P. Cates

Art Consultant: Emily Michele Cates

Printed and bound in USA

First Printing August 2020

Published by:
Cherry Creek Press
P.O. Box 2142
Los Lunas, NM 87031

I dedicate this book to my loving wife, Clara, who worked tirelessly to convert my very rough manuscript into a finished book.

I also want to gratefully acknowledge my parents, Albert and Irene, who patiently taught me morality, critical thinking and to not blindly follow the crowd.

As for my perverse sense of humor, I have no one to blame but myself.

Finally, I want to recognize my children, Alison and Emily, for whom I wrote this book in an attempt to give them an alternative to the unending leftist ideology that they are bombarded with daily.

Contents

1	The Letter to the Editor	1
2	Bertram Learns About Socialism	4
3	Bertram and the Sugar Tax	9
4	Bertram and Universal Health Care	14
5	Bertram and Antifa	17
6	Bertram Learns the Meaning of Bravery	21
7	Bertram and Free Speech	24
8	Bertram and the Senate	29
9	Bertram and the Ballot	33
10	Bertram the Activist	38
11	Bertram Finds Religion	43
12	Bertram and the Guaranteed Minimum Income	47
13	Bertram Learns About Fairness	53
14	Bertram Learns About Statistics	59
15	Bertram and the NPR Interview	65
16	Bertram and Financial Blacklisting	69
17	Bertram Interviews George Orwell	73
18	Bertram Learns a Really Big Word	77
19	Bertram and Ayn Rand's Ghost	81
20	Bertram Finds Utopia	88
21	Bertram and Diversity	93
22	Bertram and Individual Rights	99

[1]

The Letter to the Editor

THERE IS A LOT of interest in socialism these days. I don't understand the draw. To me, the best analogy between people and a socialist government is the relationship between a dog and its master. The master controls all aspects of the dog's life. If the dog is fortunate enough to have a kind, paternalistic master, he will be petted, told he is a good dog, and be allowed to sleep at the foot of the bed. If the dog has a despotic master, he will be chained in the back yard, sleep outdoors in all kinds of weather, and be beaten savagely for any mistake.

Regardless of the type of master, the dog will only receive what its master allows it to have. The dog will only eat what his master provides, when his master provides it. He will live in whatever dog house his master cares to give him. He will only be allowed to leave his yard when his master allows it and will only be allowed to socialize with dogs his master approves of. And the dog will only receive the veterinary care that his master allows it to have.

In short, the dog is totally dependent on his master for

SOCIALISM: IT'S A DOG'S LIFE

all of his needs. While the dog's life with a good master may seem a happy one, the dog is still missing one commodity that humans find essential: Freedom. Socialism seeks to provide us with the basics of life in exchange for our freedom. Doubt this? Just ask a Venezuelan.

[2]

Bertram Learns About Socialism

I WAS INCENSED BY a recent 'Letter to the Editor' in our newspaper; the very letter you in fact just read. To determine the extent of the reactionary thinking outlined in the letter, I decided to interview my dog, Bertram. Bertram is an under active Jack Russell Terrier with a bit of an independent streak. Here is the transcript of the interview.

"Hey Bertram," I said invitingly, "how about sitting down and having a little chat?"

"Okayyyy," he answered cautiously, "what about?"

"I just want to talk to you about how much you enjoy your life with me," I casually answered.

"It's okay," Bertram said as he turned to go away just a little too quickly.

"Only okay? But I give you everything you need!" I protested.

"Well, you give me most of what I need, but not necessarily what I want," Bertram said hesitantly.

"Like what?" I foolishly asked.

"Well, like food. I'm a little tired of my generic dog food. I want to eat what you eat," Bertram boldly answered.

BERTRAM LEARNS ABOUT SOCIALISM

"No way!" I responded. "People food isn't good for you. Besides I'm on a budget."

"So it's okay for you, but not for me?" Bertram countered.

"I'm only looking out for your own good. Give me another example," I demanded, hoping to get something more easily rebutted.

"I want to sleep in your bed," responded Bertram.

"But you have a nice doggie bed on the floor next to the heater," I argued.

"Yeah. On the floor," Bertram answered sardonically.

"Do you have anything productive to discuss?" I asked, getting a little irritated with his attitude.

"Health care," Bertram piped up.

"Health care?" I queried, feeling slightly confused. "I don't understand. I take you to the vet twice a year whether you need it or not."

"That's right. Health care," Bertram resolutely stated. "I want to talk about that little surprise visit to the vet last year where I lost my reproductive rights."

"Well, we all have to make sacrifices for the greater good. We can't have lots of little stray dogs running around," I reasoned.

"Who says they'll be strays? Don't you think I can take care of my own kids?" said Bertram in a wounded tone.

"Doubtful," I answered firmly. "Any other complaints?"

"Sure. I want to come and go as I please and hang out with whomever I choose," stated Bertram.

I detected a belligerent undertone in his voice. "Like who?" I asked.

"Like Butch and Wolf down the street," answered Bertram.

"Not those two Dobermans, they're deplorable! They are plotting against old man Riley!" I said in a shocked tone.

BERTRAM LEARNS ABOUT SOCIALISM

"Yep, those two. Old man Riley is a terrible master and he deserves whatever they do to him. Besides, don't you think I can think for myself?" asked Bertram.

"No I don't," I muttered under my breath, hoping he didn't hear. In an attempt to move the conversation to a more positive level, I said, "But Bertram, you love and trust me! You always call me your Beloved Leader."

"You have a problem recognizing sarcasm, don't you?" he replied.

At that point I had had enough. "Ungrateful counter revolutionary!" I screamed.

"Self serving ELITIST!" he howled.

"That's it. This interview is OVER!" I yelled.

Bertram now lives in a vacant corner of the backyard chained to a large block of concrete where he eats expired dog food. He may be re-integrated into society if he successfully completes his current re-education program and acknowledges his crimes against the people.

SOCIALISM: IT'S A DOG'S LIFE

·· [3] ··

Bertram and the Sugar Tax

BERTRAM COMPLETED his re-education program about a month ago, and while he seemed to pass with flying colors, I was still keeping a close eye on him. I had restored all his rights and privileges provisionally, contingent on his continued good behavior.

This particular balmy summer afternoon I was gazing out my front window admiring my flowers when I noticed a large crowd of neighborhood dogs and children milling around on the sidewalk in front of my house. I called Bertram. No answer. 'I better check this out,' I thought to myself.

When I reached the scene of the excitement, I found that Bertram had set up a lemonade stand. A dollar a cup. The line stretched to the end of the block.

"Hey Bertram," I said casually, "what's up with the lemonade stand?"

"I'm trying to raise a little cash to buy better doggie treats. The ones you have been feeding me taste like cardboard boiled in arsenic," he responded.

"Doesn't lemonade have a lot of sugar in it?" I asked.

"You bet!" said Bertram enthusiastically. "Why do you

SOCIALISM: IT'S A DOG'S LIFE

think it's so popular? Butch and Wolf are on their third cup."

I looked towards the end of the line, and sure enough those two reprobates were in line again.

"Well, have you ever thought about the health effects on your customers from all that sugar? They can develop diabetes, become obese, and get cavities and even tummy aches. I think you should set aside a portion of your profits to help your customers pay for their future treatments. I'm thinking 80 cents a cup should be about right."

"But after the costs of my raw materials that only leaves me one cent per cup in profit. It is hardly worth the effort!" he protested.

"Bertram," I said sternly, "don't tell me have you forgotten your re-education lessons. Remember, profiting from your fellow creatures is immoral and selfish. You should start enterprises for the sole purpose of serving your community, not enriching yourself. Do you need to go back to re-education camp?"

"No, I see your point," Bertram responded dejectedly.

"Good. I'm glad you agree. Now open up that cash box so I can collect the first installment of the sugar tax." I grabbed a couple handfuls of cash and headed back to the house.

After about an hour I decided that it was time to collect the second installment. I went outside, but saw Bertram alone at his stand. There was no line, and he had no customers. He had raised the price of the lemonade to $2 a cup.

"Where are all your customers?" I asked.

"They left. Nobody was willing to pay $2 for a cup of lemonade," he said sadly.

"Well I don't blame them. That's price gouging!"

"I guess I'll close up shop and go back inside," he said

BERTRAM AND THE SUGAR TAX

despondently with his tail tucked between his short little legs. He took down his stand and hauled it, along with three gallons of unsold lemonade, back to the house.

"Bertram, let this be a lesson to you," I said when we were back inside. "What just happened to you is so typical of the misery caused by unregulated capitalism. This is why the government must tightly control the markets."

Bertram did not respond. He was staring at the nickel and three pennies in his cash box.

BERTRAM AND THE SUGAR TAX

·· [4] ··

Bertram and Universal Health Care

I WAS WATCHING TV when Bertram, my Jack Russell, came unsteadily into the living room. "What's up pup?" I said. "You don't look so good."

"I don't feel so hot. I have a tummy ache, and I think I need to go to the vet," he groaned.

"I'm not surprised, after you drank all three gallons of your left over lemonade! I'll call Dr. Wurst."

"Oh no, not Dr. Wurst!" cried Bertram. "He is the worst. He still uses a rear entry thermometer. And it's really old and really big and really cold. Can't we use a little of that sugar tax money and go to a decent vet?"

"Sorry Bertram," I commiserated, "revenues didn't meet expectations, so I had to cancel the program."

"What!" he said. "So, after all the sugar tax I paid I don't get any benefits?"

"Wait a minute!" I snapped. "This is your fault. If you had worked harder to sell the rest of that lemonade there would have been enough money to properly fund the universal health care program. Remember your re-education classes. 'To each according to his needs, from each according to his ability.' You

BERTRAM AND UNIVERSAL HEALTH CARE

SOCIALISM: IT'S A DOG'S LIFE

didn't run your lemonade business to the best of your ability, so needs were not met. Your mismanagement and greed cost the entire community a much needed program! Do you need to go back to re-education camp to review this?"

"No, I guess you're right," he admitted. "Let's forget about the vet."

Bertram then looked up and noticed the TV for the first time. "Is that new?" he asked.

"It is!" I said proudly. "When revenues for the universal health care program didn't meet expectations, I transferred the money into the education budget. We can now enrich our lives by watching informative and enlightened programming."

"What are you watching?" asked Bertram.

"A fascinating program about the metaphysical ethos of medieval South Asian religions and their parallels with modern collectivism."

"Can we watch *Lassie* instead?"

"No!" I replied. "*Lassie* is a crass commercial program designed to take the masses' minds off their capitalism induced misery!"

"Well, how about *Wishbone*?"

"*Wishbone* does have some low grade educational benefits, but it falls well short of the higher plane of enlightenment that I have in mind for us."

"Never mind," Bertram said. "I have a headache now. I think I'll just go take a nap in my doggie bed. You know, the one on the floor."

I was feeling very self satisfied with how I had expanded Bertram's horizons as I nodded off during the second half of that fascinating program on the metaphysical ethos of medieval South Asian religions and their parallels with modern collectivism.

[5]

Bertram and Antifa

MY LITTLE DOG, Betram, was on his way downtown to withdraw a little walking around money from his account at the local branch of Pet Deposit Savings and Loan when he ran into what appeared to be a riot. At one end of Main Street masked individuals armed with batons and bricks were attacking a free speech rally. At the other end, masked individuals were chasing frightened old men down the street, and in the middle, cars with conservative bumper stickers were being burned.

Being a Jack Russell, Bertram didn't have enough sense to be afraid. He walked up to the nearest masked man and asked, "Hey, what are you guys up to here?"

"We are Antifa," answered the masked man, as though that explained everything.

It didn't for Bertram. "Antifa?" he mused. "Aren't you missing a couple of letters like an 'r' and a 't'?"

"No, you don't understand. Antifa stands for 'anti-fascists.'"

"What's a fascist?" asked Bertram.

The masked man explained. "Fascists are horrible people who try to control other people by violently attacking

SOCIALISM: IT'S A DOG'S LIFE

opposition rallies, destroying private property, and physically intimidating those who don't agree with them."

"Isn't that what you are doing?" Bertram pointed out.

"No, you have entirely missed the point. We are social minded activists who use violence merely as a tool to draw attention to the plight of the oppressed people."

"Walk, quack, duck," Bertram muttered.

"What did you say?" demanded the masked man in a threatening manner.

"Oh nothing, just trying to remember my password," Bertram replied mildly. "Say, do you mind lending me your brick? I have a plight or two back at home that I would like to draw attention to."

"Sure, help yourself," the masked man said obligingly.

* * *

I was watching enlightened educational TV when Bertram returned from the bank.

"Hey!" he yelled. "My pet brick and I want to have a discussion with you about your fascist control of this household!"

"I'm not a fascist, I'm a socialist," I said, correcting him.

"What's the difference?"

"It is very simple, I responded. "A fascist seeks to control people through violence whereas a socialist seeks to do it through education."

Bertram seemed confused. "Education?" he asked.

"Sure. Like that re-education camp you attended a few months ago."

"Seemed more like propaganda to me," Bertram noted.

"No, it was clearly education."

"What's the difference?"

"Education is what we socialists use and propaganda is what our opposition uses. Is that clear?"

"Crystal," answered Bertram doubtfully. "By the way, just in case this comes up, my pet brick and I had absolutely nothing to do with the large crack in your windshield. And Butch and Wolf did not egg me on."

And there it was. Those two deplorable Dobermans again.

·· [6] ··

Bertram Learns the Meaning of Bravery

Bertram, my little dog, and I were watching the local news on our new educational TV. The newscast broke away to cover a developing story. A couple of dozen protesters had surrounded the house of a local newspaper columnist and were banging on the doors and windows screaming obscenities and threats.

"I don't understand what is going on," Bertram mused. "Why are those people attacking that house?"

"It's like this," I explained, "those brave protesters are expressing their outrage at the counter revolutionary content of the latest column written by the man who lives in that house."

"So the protestors are brave?" Bertram asked.

"Very!" I replied admiringly.

"How many people are in the house?"

"Four," I answered. "The columnist, his wife, and their two young children."

"So are the columnist's friends on their way to help beat up the protesters?"

"No, of course not. They could be thrown in jail for that," I said.

SOCIALISM: IT'S A DOG'S LIFE

BERTRAM LEARNS THE MEANING OF BRAVERY

"So are the police going to come over and bust the protesters' heads and haul them off to jail?" he persisted.

"No way. The police are just going to stand by and watch. They don't want to be the reason this peaceful protest turns violent."

"Seems kind of violent to me," Bertram opined. "So the protesters outnumber the dastardly columnist 25 to 1, and the police aren't going to do anything to stop them."

"That's right," I said.

"And the protesters are very brave?" Bertram said, more as a question than a statement.

"That's right," I said, feeling a little unsure of myself now. "They are brave because they are not afraid to express their beliefs regardless of the consequences."

"Seems like the only one suffering any consequences is the columnist," Bertram remarked as he jumped off the couch.

"Where are you going?" I demanded.

"I going to get my pet brick, and then Butch and Wolf and I are going to go down and have a peaceful discussion with those brave protesters. And there will be consequences."

I shuddered. Those deplorable dogs, Butch and Wolf, again. How I hate them.

· · [7] · ·

Bertram and Free Speech

Bertram had finally prevailed upon me to let him watch *Wishbone* on my new educational TV. He grinned and wagged his tail throughout the program. It was good to see him enjoying something educational for a change.

When the program ended I switched to the local news. The reporter was covering a protest at the local university, Y.U. State. Bertram watched in fascination as one group of students started shoving students from the other group and ripping up their signs.

"Why are those students attacking the other students?" he asked.

"The students with the signs are supporting a planned free speech rally on campus," I explained.

"So why are the other students attacking them?" asked Bertram. "I thought free speech was a constitutional right."

"First of all, the Constitution is an outdated racist document. Secondly, you have to understand that free speech rallies are really just an opportunity for rabid counter revolutionaries to spread their propaganda. The brave socialist students won't allow that to happen," I further explained.

"So these socialist students are brave in the same way as the protesters at the columnist's house were?"

"Yes, and they ARE brave!" I replied in an irritated tone.

"But they are against free speech," Bertram pointed out.

"Okay, I see that you have once again forgotten a part of your re-education training. Free speech is a very powerful tool, so powerful in fact that a well ordered society cannot afford to let subversive groups have access to it. So the brave socialist students aren't against free speech that is used in a responsible manner; just the free speech of the other students."

"Who decides which groups are subversive?" inquired Bertram.

"The government of course! Have you forgotten everything? I'm beginning to think that you need to go back to re-education camp for a refresher course."

"I remember from re-education history class that in pre-enlightened times the brave freedom loving socialists were regarded as subversive. Did they have free speech then?" he persisted.

I was losing patience with this line of reasoning. "Bertram," I said, "you cannot apply the standards of yesterday to today."

"So that's a yes?" Bertram continued with a slight smirk on his face.

"Your doggie treat allotment has just been reduced by half. Do you want to try for 75%?" I retorted.

Bertram hung his head and gave me those soulful puppy dog eyes. "No, I'm sorry. I know you are only trying to properly educate me, but these are complicated subjects and I'm not all that smart. I am just a little dog after all."

I relented. "Okay, you can have your treats back, but be more careful about what you say from now on."

"Thanks!" he replied gratefully as he headed for the front door.

SOCIALISM: IT'S A DOG'S LIFE

"Where are you going?" I asked.

"I'm going to practice proper free speech on Butch and Wolf. That should shut them up."

'That will not end well,' I thought to myself as I looked up Dr. Wurst's phone number.

·· [8] ··

Bertram and the Senate

It was a lazy Sunday morning. I was drinking a cup of fair trade coffee and looking through yesterday's mail when a mailer from my political party caught my eye. Just then Bertram came down for breakfast.

He stretched and yawned. "Morning!" he greeted. "What's for breakfast?"

"Generic dog food. It's already in your bowl."

"No surprise there," he mumbled and then proceeded to dispatch his meal in record time.

When he finished he looked up and asked, "What are you reading?"

"Just a mailer from my political party, the Party of Obedient People."

Bertram chuckled, "The POOP party?"

"No, the POP party. You don't include 'of's' and 'the's' in acronyms. This mailer is on a very important topic. The POP party is launching a campaign to do away with the Senate."

Bertram appeared to be deep in thought for a few seconds. "Isn't the Senate in the Constitution? Oh, by the way, where does the POOP party stand on the sugar tax?" he inquired.

SOCIALISM: IT'S A DOG'S LIFE

"Very funny," I said, and then continued, "I already explained to you that the Constitution is an outdated and racist document. The Senate is one of the outdated parts."

"How?" he asked.

"It is undemocratic. The Senate gives equal representation to each state, regardless of the population of that state. The result is that states with small populations have more power per capita than states with large populations." I was feeling quite proud of myself for putting it so succinctly that even Bertram should understand it.

"But we live in a state with a small population. Why should we want to change it?"

"Bertram, just because it benefits us doesn't make it right. We have to sacrifice for the common good."

"Oh," he said.

"Just 'Oh'? No smart aleck come back?" I challenged.

"Just 'Oh,'" said Bertram. "I am taking your advice from our free speech discussion to heart."

I knew I was going to regret this, but I was dying to know what counter argument he could possibly make against my superior logic.

"Okay, I'll suspend the rules against dangerous speech for five minutes. What are you thinking?"

"Well," Bertram started reluctantly, "isn't the House of Representatives proportioned by population."

"Yes."

"So don't the larger states have more power than smaller states in the House?"

"What is your point?" I said brusquely, not wanting to concede anything at this point.

"Remember that I am just a little dog and don't have your mighty cognitive powers," he continued respectfully, "but it

seems to me that the Senate protects the people in the small states from being forced to do things they don't want to do by people in the bigger states. Sort of like an anti-bully police force."

"Well, really!" I said. "That's your argument? Don't you know that the population centers in the large states are the source of all the best and most progressive socialist ideas? It's people in the small states that are using the Senate to block the inevitable social progress that will come from those ideas. As if they should even have a say in this. This obstructionism must stop and the best way to do it is to abolish the Senate!"

"But, ..." Bertram began.

"That's enough out of you. Your five minutes are over."

[9]

Bertram and the Ballot

A COUPLE WEEKS HAD passed since Bertram's and my discussion on the Senate. As I sipped my fair trade cup of coffee on a dreary stormy day that caused clouds to be reflected in my black coffee, Bertram entered the room.

"Morning," he said.

"Good morning to you!" I answered.

"What are you reading?" he inquired.

"It's a sample ballot for next week's election. Want to see it?"

"Sure. I haven't decided how to vote yet."

I handed over the form and Bertram studied it for a few minutes. "All the candidates are from the POOP party. Didn't any other parties run candidates?" he asked.

"POP party. And yes, other parties submitted candidates but they didn't make it past the review committee."

"What review committee?"

"The Committee to Ensure Enlightened Candidates. All potential candidates have to pass review by that committee. We know that the electorate doesn't have time to properly screen the candidates themselves, so the committee ensures that only right minded candidates with the proper enlightened views are allowed on the ballot. We wouldn't want the electorate to make any more mistakes," I explained carefully.

"Wow, I better let Butch and Wolf know right away!" Bertram said. "They just started a new party and want to get some candidates on the ballot."

"What is their party's name?" I asked, pretending to be helpful.

"National Association of Dogs."

"So NADs for short," I said, taking advantage of the opportunity to avenge the endless POOP party comments.

"That's right, how did you know?"

"What is their platform?" I asked, ignoring the obvious.

"They are opposed to the neutering laws."

"Anything else?"

"Yeah, they promise a Milk-Bone in every bowl," Bertram responded, "and something besides generic dog food on the weekends."

"Do they have a campaign slogan?" I asked, fearing what the answer might be.

"Of course, do you think they are amateurs? It's 'Jump on Our Band Waggin.'"

"Waggin'. Cute. I was afraid that given the party name and platform, the deplorable Dobermans would have used the slogan as an opportunity for a crude joke."

"Nope, they're legit!" Bertram said proudly. "I can get a list of candidates over to the committee after lunch."

"Too late," I smirked. "The deadline to submit candidates was 60 days ago."

Bertram looked devastated. "Why did you have me go through all this if it was too late?" he asked in a voice dripping with accusation.

"I just wanted to see where you would go with it," I said.

SOCIALISM: IT'S A DOG'S LIFE

Bertram headed out the doggie door.

"You are about to find out. I am going to deposit some of your party members around the back yard. Have fun finding them," he said as the flap slapped his behind.

[10]

Bertram the Activist

Having finished my cup of fair trade cofeee, I called out to my little Jack Russell, "Bertram! Come here. It's time to clip your toenails." There followed no scurrying of little escaping feet or muffled howls of protest; just silence. 'Where can that little dog be?' I thought as I started to compose an appropriately themed children's song in my head. 'I better go find him.'

I stepped outside and looked in the direction of old man Riley's house, the abode of the deplorable Dobermans, Butch and Wolf. Bertram and the deplorables stood on the sidewalk next to a sign. I walked down to them to better read the sign.

"What are you three up to?" I asked.

"We are taking donations for a new charity Butch and Wolf just started called Paternity Rights for Pups!" Bertram answered excitedly. "Scientific study has shown that positive male role models are crucial in the social development of young dogs, and we want to provide travel assistance to low income doggie daddies so they can visit their offspring."

"Very commendable," I said approvingly. "But Bertram, this doesn't help you. You can't have puppies."

"Yes, I know, and thanks for that by the way. I still want to help out in a good cause. Anyway, Butch and Wolf both have puppies."

"Really?" I asked. "How many?"

"Hey Wolf," Bertram hollered, "how many pups do you have?"

"Five."

"And you Butch?"

"Six or twelve."

"Aren't you sure?" Bertram asked.

"Well, I think Fifi may have been fooling around on me with the collie next door," Butch answered. "She always had a thing for Lassie and that last litter had the woolliest Dobermans you ever saw."

"Lassie was a bitch," I stated.

"Sure, but aren't all movie stars?" Butch replied ruefully.

"No, not that kind of bitch. She was a bitch as in a female dog," I elaborated.

Bertram started giggling.

"What's so funny?" I demanded indignantly.

"Oh, that's alright," Butch said charitably. "Fifi always was a free spirit. That's what I love about her."

In an effort to change the subject I asked, "How much money have you raised?"

Bertram looked in the jar. "Not much; just three dollars and twenty-seven cents."

"Well, that won't get Butch and Wolf many bus tickets," I observed.

"It's not for them. They always travel by plane. They're show dogs," Bertram said.

I decided to help them out with some useful advice. "If you really want to have a successful charity you need to get

BERTRAM THE ACTIVIST

the government involved. If you are very convincing you may even get it upgraded to an entitlement, and then you will have access to an unlimited amount of other people's money."

I had Bertram's interest. "How do you do that?" he asked.

"It's simple. You just lobby your congressmen."

"How do you do that?"

"The most effective way is to chase them down in elevators or at restaurants, and then scream at them until they give into your demands."

"Won't that just make them mad?" reasoned Bertram.

"No. They always cave if you yell loud and long enough. Most of them are 'Flakes.'"

Bertram considered this for a minute. Then he shouted at the deplorables, "Butch, Wolf, grab your signs. Let's go find Senator Bassett and hound him!"

I couldn't help feeling a touch of pride in my little doggie activist as he and his posse disappeared into the sunset.

·· [11] ··

Bertram Finds Religion

It was a clear and cool fall day. I was savoring the view of the leaves changing colors around the distant tenements while I sipped my fair trade coffee. The Sunday edition of *The New York Times* lay folded on my lap, inspiring daydreams of utopian workers' paradises, where intellectuals were rightfully worshipped for their vision and compassion.

This endearing fantasy was interrupted by Bertram's sudden entrance into the kitchen. He was wearing his best collar. It was made of braided leather with a turquoise clasp; like a little doggie bolo tie.

"Going out?" I asked pleasantly.

"Yes I am. Butch and Wolf are taking me to their church today. They're deacons!"

The mention of the deplorable Dobermans did not brighten my mood.

"I'm surprised that any church would allow those two in," I said. "Besides, I didn't know that dogs were religious."

"But we are," Bertram protested. "Don't you know dog spelled backwards is God?"

I ignored that platitude. "What is the name of their church?"

SOCIALISM: IT'S A DOG'S LIFE

"*Denominational Order of God*. We are in favor of greater religious freedom for all of God's canines. And we are against cats."

"You mean nondenominational, not denominational. And what's wrong with cats? They are cute and cuddly. You should let them into your church."

"No, denominational is correct. We are against demons too. And as for the cats, we'll let cats in when humans let grizzly bears into their churches," Bertram countered.

I shook my head. "Cats and grizzly bears aren't the same thing," I pointed out.

"Oh yes they are," Bertram argued. "They are both mean, aggressive, filthy, hairy animals. And their litter boxes stink."

"Bears don't have litter boxes," I replied blandly.

"Of course they do!" Bertram responded. "They are called 'the woods'. But it's Sunday so let's put our differences aside. You should come with us," Bertram offered.

"No thanks," I declined, "I don't approve of religion."

"Why not?"

"It is the opium of the masses."

Bertram looked puzzled. "What does perfume have to do with religion?"

"Not *Opium* the perfume, opium the drug," I said.

"Still not following."

"Look," I explained, "religion misleads people into putting their hopes for justice and prosperity in some mythical super-being instead of where it belongs."

"Where does it belong?" Bertram asked.

"In government of course; government is the answer to everything!"

"Sounds like you worship government," Bertram observed.

That hit a nerve. "My faith in the ability of government

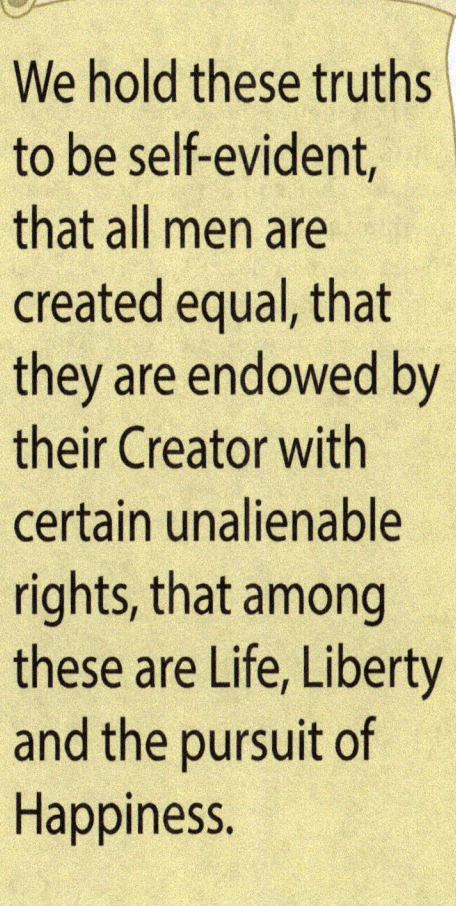

to overcome every obstacle, to right every wrong, to create a heaven on earth in no way constitutes a religion!"

"Okay, calm down. I am sorry I said that," Bertram responded, backpedaling in the face of my righteous indignation.

"And that's not all!" I continued. "Religion misleads people into believing that their rights come from God!"

"They don't?" gasped Bertram.

"Of course not; they come from the government! And I'll tell you something else . . . "

Just then the doorbell rang. "Gotta run!" Bertram called out as he raced for the door and salvation.

"This discussion isn't over, little dog," I grimly said to myself.

·· [12] ··

Bertram and the Guaranteed Minimum Income

It was a cold and grey December morning. I watched as the wind blew swirls of snow around the distant tenements. Fortunately, in my house a cozy fire kept my living room warm and cheery. I sipped my fair trade coffee, reading the latest mailer from the POP party. Bertram was stretched out in front of the fireplace, with his head between his paws, contentedly absorbing as much heat from the fire as possible.

"Bertram," I said, "you should read this latest POP party mailer."

Bertram lifted his head and yawned. "Why?" he asked. "What is the POOP party up to now?"

"The POP party," I corrected him. "Anyway, this is great news. After months of agitation on my part, they are finally throwing their full weight behind the GMI!"

"That is great news," agreed Bertram. "Everyone should be allowed to shop on TV."

I grimaced. The memory of the surprise delivery of two crates of specialty doggie treats last month was still painful. "No, GMI stands for Guaranteed Minimum Income. Also, you are still forbidden from watching that channel."

SOCIALISM: IT'S A DOG'S LIFE

BERTRAM AND THE GUARANTEED MINIMUM INCOME

Bertram laid his head back on his paws and closed his eyes.

"Aren't you going to ask me what GMI is?" I asked, surprised by his uncharacteristic lack of curiosity.

"No."

"Well, I'll tell you anyway. GMI is a program where everyone is guaranteed a living wage, whether they work or not."

Bertram raised one eyelid, started to say something, thought better of it, and closed his eyes again.

"Come on, out with it," I ordered.

"Okay. How are you going to pay for this?"

"Oh, that's easy," I said. "We will just raise taxes on businesses and the rich. Anyway, it isn't fair that they have so much more than the less fortunate."

Bertram considered this for a moment. "That didn't work out so well when you imposed a sugar tax on my lemonade stand," he observed.

"Bertram, how many times do we have to go over this? The fiscal failure of the universal health care program was your fault. Even though I left you a penny a cup profit you greedily increased the price of lemonade out of the reach of the common creature, and your business failed as a result. It is the duty of every business person to manage their business in such a way as to maximize the resources available for the common good."

"Right," Bertram said in the tone that screamed 'wrong'.

"Besides," I continued undeterred, "the GMI will ensure that everyone receives a fair and livable wage. Just think of the money we will save on welfare, food stamps, social security, and unemployment benefits. Why this program will almost pay for itself!"

"The problem lies in the definition of 'almost'," Bertram

commented dryly, and then added, "Just a thought. Won't people stop working and paying taxes if they can stay home and collect a guaranteed income? This reminds me of a parable from Butch's and Wolf's bible school class; 'Give a man a fish and you feed him for a day, teach a man to fish and you feed him for a lifetime, promise a man a free fish everyday and he will vote for you forever.'"

"That last part of the parable is not in the Bible," I said accusingly.

"Not in your species-centric Bible, but it is in ours. You'll find it in the 'Gospel of Saint Bernard.'"

"Well you must have a very low opinion of your fellow creatures if you believe they are only motivated by greed and self-interest," I chided. "The POP party believes that people are motivated by love of community and will happily work to the best of their ability for the common good as long as they have enough to eat and a roof over their heads. Besides," I expounded, warming up to my current favorite topic, "those who choose not to work will ignite an artistic renaissance when their creativity is freed from the tyranny of work."

"Can I get a GMI?" Bertram inquired as he sat up. He suddenly seemed a little more interested.

"What do you think you're getting now?" I retorted. "You eat and live in my house, and you don't do anything to earn it."

"That's not true," Bertram answered in a hurt tone. "I provide guard dog services and companionship in return for my keep."

I got up and put on my coat. The fire had gone out, and I was late for the weekly POP party Executive Board meeting. "I'll see you tonight. Be a good dog while I'm gone," I said.

* * *

BERTRAM AND THE GUARANTEED MINIMUM INCOME

Later that evening I laid in my bed reading a fascinating book from the POP party required reading list about mobilizing social consciousness among the masses. Bertram was sound asleep in his doggie bed on the floor by the heater. Suddenly, I heard the front door knob jiggling like someone was trying to break in. "Bertram," I whispered, "go see if someone is trying to break into the house."

Bertram opened one eye and studied me for a second. "No thanks. I'm taking that GMI. My creativity is blossoming as we speak."

SOCIALISM: IT'S A DOG'S LIFE

· · [13] · ·

Bertram Learns About Fairness

It was a glorious late spring day. The sun was beaming down on the Earth. The flowers were smiling back in appreciation. Butterflies were dancing from be-petalled face to be-petalled face, kissing each in turn, while the bumblebees beat out an ode to beauty with their wings. I surveyed this wondrous scene, so vividly framed by the dark distant tenements, while I sipped my fair trade coffee. The latest mailer from the POP party was lying on my lap.

Bertram came lazily downstairs for his breakfast. As he passed me on the way to his doggie bowl, he noticed the mailer.

"That's the ugliest dog I've ever seen," he announced, pointing at the top of the mailer with his nose.

"That's not a dog, it's a hyena. It's the POP party's mascot. We selected the hyena because it is a highly social and misunderstood animal, just like us."

"Don't hyenas gang up on other creatures and steal their food?" Bertram asked.

"Where did you hear such a counter revolutionary lie?" I snapped.

SOCIALISM: IT'S A DOG'S LIFE

BERTRAM LEARNS ABOUT FAIRNESS

"It was on a recent episode of *Lassie*. She bravely fought off a huge mob of hysterical hyenas that were trying to steal food from a family of African Hunting Dogs. It was also on *The Lion King*," Bertram replied with authority.

"Well those are just mean spirited caricatures. They aren't fair at all."

"Is it fair when they beat up other creatures and steal their food? The hyenas didn't work for that food. It reminds me of one of the parables in the *Denominational Order of God* bible."

I groaned.

Bertram continued, "It is the parable of the little red hen. She did all this work to grow wheat, mill it into flour, and bake it into bread. At each step she asked the other animals to help, but they refused. When the bread was ready all the animals showed up to eat it, but she wouldn't share. I think the other animals were hyenas."

"Wait here, I'll be right back," I said. I went into my den and brought back a copy of the POP party's *Enlightened Fables*. "Look on page 37," I said, handing the book to Bertram.

Bertram read the ending out loud, "And the little red hen shared the bread with all the other animals, and she received the Workers' Hero Medal for her efforts."

"They left out a part," Bertram observed.

"What's that?"

"And she never made bread again."

"That's just not true!" I stated. "She would have happily fulfilled her responsibility to the community to work to the best of her ability to satisfy the needs of the other animals. Besides, if she refused, she would be socially shamed and the animals would find another little red hen. There are always more little red hens."

Bertram sighed heavily. He was obviously not convinced.

SOCIALISM: IT'S A DOG'S LIFE

"Okay, how about the parable of the ants and the grasshopper?" he said.

"Another one of your *D.O.G.* bible stories?" I asked, with more than a hint of sarcasm.

"Well it's better than the *Church of Anarchy and Terrorism* bible," he retorted. "And yes, it is. It is the story of the ants who worked all summer to stockpile food for the winter while the grasshopper played and played, and did no work. When winter hit the grasshopper starved to death."

"Firstly, stop dissing cats. Secondly, look at page 93 of the book I just gave you," I instructed.

Bertram turned to the assigned page and read aloud, "And the ants shared their food with the grasshopper and everyone was happy in their socialist utopian society."

"They forgot a part again," Bertram mused. Then added, "And since they had to feed the lazy grasshopper they ran out of food before the winter ended, and they all died of starvation."

"That won't happen as long as there are enough ants," I pointed out.

"But what if the ants get tired of working to feed the lazy grasshopper and decide to sit around, waiting for someone else to feed them?" he asked.

"That won't happen. The ants will not be allowed to stop working to support the grasshopper," I rationalized.

"How are you going to make them work?"

"I don't want to go into that in that story. It may frighten the children," I replied.

(Editor's note: Dear reader, if you are curious as to the methods not detailed above, I recommend that you read two of George Orwell's books; Animal Farm and Nineteen Eighty-Four.)

BERTRAM LEARNS ABOUT FAIRNESS

"You know, your POOP party fables are very unfair," Bertram said.

I was angered by this. "You know what isn't fair?" I stated, my voice building to a crescendo of righteous indignation. "It isn't fair that some have too much and others have too little! Everyone should have the same!"

Bertram glanced around the house and then gazed out the window. "You have a lot more than the people who live in those tenements," he observed. "Shouldn't you invite some of them to live with you to make it fairer?"

"Bertram," I tried to explain, "my duties on the POP party General Planning and Implementation Subcommittee of the Executive Board are so crucial to the achievement of a socialist utopia that I cannot be distracted by petty day to day concerns. I have to have this standard of living so that I can give to the community to the best of my abilities. Do you understand?"

"Sure," answered Bertram. "I have a pretty good idea of fairness now."

· · [14] · ·

Bertram Learns About Statistics

BERTRAM AND I were sitting on the couch watching an enlightened POP party approved newscast on my new educational TV set. The host was discussing the skyrocketing rate of sexual assaults being perpetrated against young women on American campuses.

"Wow! A third of all women attending college will suffer sexual assault during their time in college. That's horrifying," I said.

"That's bad, but not as bad as cat assaults against dogs. Did you know that 67 percent of all dogs have been assaulted by cats? That is CAT-a-strophic."

"That doesn't sound right. Where did you get that number?"

"At last night's local chapter meeting of National Association of Dogs. We held it at Butch's and Wolf's place. Butch and I have both suffered from cat assaults. So that's two out of three, two-thirds of dogs."

"There is a problem with your figures," I observed.

"Well, I did round up to the next whole number to get the 67%," Bertram conceded.

"That's not what I meant. Your sample size is way too small to be statistically relevant."

Bertram looked uncomfortable. "Sample size?" he asked hesitatingly.

"Yes, sample size. The number of dogs you interviewed is your sample size. You only interviewed three."

"Oh, I'm glad you clarified that," Bertram said with a look of relief on his face.

I could tell that Dr. Wurst had loomed large in his imagination.

"How many should I interview?" he inquired.

"I think that there must be millions of dogs in this country. I'm not a statistician, but I'm guessing that you would need a few thousand dogs to have a representative sample."

"That sounds like a lot," Bertram said.

* * *

About a month later I found Bertram hard at work near his doggie bed on the floor next to the heater. He had a pencil tucked under one ear, and was pounding away on a calculator with one paw while he shifted through a stack of papers with the other. He noticed me staring at him and said, "Oh, hi. I took your advice and significantly expanded my sample size."

"Really? How many?"

"3,637. The numbers are even worse than I thought. 79 percent of all dogs have suffered from cat assaults!"

"Well, that does sound like a decent sample size, but I still have a problem with your figures."

Bertram looked concerned and then went back to pounding his calculator.

"You're right!" he exclaimed. "I did have an error in my

BERTRAM LEARNS ABOUT STATISTICS

math. Actually, 98 percent of all dogs have been assaulted by cats!"

"I detect a bias in your sampling methodology," I stated flatly. Bertram looked dazed and confused, so I continued, taking advantage of his temporary loss for words. "To be statistically relevant, samples must be random. Where did you get your data?"

"From several FIDO centers all around the country."

"What are those?"

"It stands for Feline Induced Dog Outrages. They are support groups for dogs that have suffered from abuse at the paws of cats."

"Don't you think that only interviewing dogs who have been abused skews your data, rendering your statistics incorrect?"

"What should I do?" he asked.

"Collect your data in a random and scientific manner."

Bertram looked as if the task ahead was overwhelming.

"Good," I said to myself, "that should end this ludicrous endeavor."

* * *

A couple of months later, I again saw Bertram hard at work near his doggie bed on the floor next to the heater. He was really working hard this time. He had on green eyeshades, had a huge pile of paper in front of him, and was studiously tapping away on a calculator with a long paper tape stretched out halfway across the room.

"What are you up to now?"

"I took an online course on beginning statistics at Dog U., and I am redoing the cat assault study."

SOCIALISM: IT'S A DOG'S LIFE

BERTRAM LEARNS ABOUT STATISTICS

"Really? What is your sample size?"

"10,531," Bertram said proudly.

"Wow. That is a pretty impressive number. What were your sampling techniques?"

"I conducted interviews on the streets and by phone, and I mailed out questionnaires to dogs around the country. I retained Fluffy, the tabby next door, as a consultant to ensure my methods were proper."

"Sounds like you did everything right. What are your results?"

"I'm just finishing it up now," he said, as he pushed buttons for a couple more minutes and then announced, "53 percent of all dogs have suffered from cat abuse."

"I stand corrected," I said. "I didn't believe your premise at first, but your methods seem sound. I guess that cat abuse really is a serious problem for dogs. 53 percent is a lot of scratching!"

"It's not just scratching!" Bertram exclaimed excitedly. "There is also hissing and dirty looks. My research found that six percent of dogs suffer from cat scratches, 15 percent from hissing, and 32 percent suffer from dirty looks. Cats live for dirty looks."

I buried my head in my hands. "Bertram, I don't even know where to start."

"I do! Start getting rid of cats!"

SOCIALISM: IT'S A DOG'S LIFE

· · [15] · ·

Bertram and the NPR Interview

AT EXACTLY 10:07 A.M., Libby Real welcomed Bertram to her radio show. "Good morning. This is your host, Libby Real, and welcome to this episode of *Why Conservatives are Always Wrong*. My guest today is Mr. Bertram J. Russell. Welcome to the show Mr. Russell."

"Good morning Lib. Nice to be here, and please call me Bertram."

"You may address me as Libby or Ms. Real," the host retorted coldly.

"Okay," Bertram said agreeably, "let's keep it Real!"

Ms. Real's scowl was palpable, even over the radio. "Very well, Mr. Russell. I invited you here to discuss your inexplicable hatred of cats."

"Oh, it's very explicable!" Bertram explicated. "Cats are mean, sneaky, smelly, hairy beasts!"

"Mr. Russell, that is pure unadulterated prejudice. Shame on you! And your rabid hatred doesn't stop there. You have been quoted as saying that all cats should be fed to grizzly bears. How do you respond to that?"

"Well, first off Libby, there is no rabid anything. Here, check

SOCIALISM: IT'S A DOG'S LIFE

BERTRAM AND THE NPR INTERVIEW

out my collar. All my shots are up to date," he said, holding his tags out for her to see.

"And," Bertram continued, "I don't advocate feeding cats to grizzly bears. That would be cannibalism."

Ms. Real continued her assault. "Furthermore you have... wait... what?... cannibalism? Cats and grizzly bears are not the same thing!"

"Seems like I have had this conversation before," Bertram said. "And yes they are!"

(Editor's note: Dear reader, at this point please refer back to Chapter 11. It will save me a lot of typing.)

At the conclusion of the conversation on the cat vs. grizzly bear controversy, Ms. Real made a valiant attempt to get the interview back on track. "Mr. Russell, isn't it true that you belong to a counter revolutionary organization known as the National Association of Dogs, and that that organization advocates for the removal of all cats from this country?"

"That's right," Bertram volunteered. "And we even have a chant. Go Na... "

Ms. Real swiftly cut him off. "We will have none of that language on this program!"

"... tional Association of Dogs, go." Bertram trailed off. "Where are you getting all this stuff from, anyway?" Bertram inquired.

"Why, from a most reliable source; The Party of Obedient People."

"Ah, the POOP party. I should have known," Bertram said. "By the way, did the POOP party tell you that 53 percent of all dogs suffer from cat assaults, and that the POOP party's mascot is a miserable hyena!"

SOCIALISM: IT'S A DOG'S LIFE

"Mr. Russell, please do not continue with your habitual maligning of the enlightened and socially minded POP party. It will not be tolerated here. As for your obviously made up statistics on cat assaults, let me remind you that you will not be allowed to play the victim on this show. My role here is to expose you for the scoundrel you are and to brow beat and demonize you."

"I am not a cat!" snarled Bertram.

"What does that even mean?"

"I don't use a litter box."

"Is that a threat?"

"Not anymore!" Bertram responded as he leapt off his chair and hiked his leg over Ms. Real's shoe.

Ms. Real's screams were palpable. Even over the radio.

·· [16] ··

Bertram and Financial Blacklisting

I WAS BUSY SETTING out snacks and an assortment of herbal teas and fair trade coffees when the doorbell rang. Bertram jumped off his favorite perch on the back of the couch and ran to the front door, hurling incomprehensible threats and insults at the potential intruder. I ran to the door, restrained Bertram, and opened the door. My good friend and fellow POP party Executive Board member, Libby Real, walked in.

"Good morning Libby, glad to see you. The others should be here shortly," I affably greeted her, all the while retaining a tight grip on Bertram's collar.

"Good morning!" she replied. "And Bertram, I hope we can make up after that somewhat confrontational interview the other day." She bent down to pat his head. Bertram growled lowly, gazing with malicious intent at her open toed sandals.

"Don't even think about it!" I cautioned. "Now sit down and be a good dog while Libby and I conduct our business." Bertram returned to his favorite perch and continued to growl in a low and threatening manner.

"I brought a new list of targets for our financial blacklisting operations," Libby said, generously helping herself to

SOCIALISM: IT'S A DOG'S LIFE

BERTRAM AND FINANCIAL BLACKLISTING

a pile of cheese and crackers and a steaming cup of catmint herbal tea.

"Oh good!" I replied enthusiastically. "Since our initial efforts to get the credit card companies to stop doing business with our first listing of counter revolutionaries was so successful, I want to extend the program to the major banks."

(Editor's note: Dear reader, financial blacklisting is not a figment of the author's imagination. It is a real program, and several major credit card companies have participated in financial blacklisting of certain individuals and groups based primarily on those individuals' or groups' political beliefs.)

Bertram had stopped growling and was listening intently. Discussions concerning money always had this effect on him. "What's financial blacklisting?" he asked.

Libby rushed to explain, "We provide the credit card companies with a list of names of people and groups whose beliefs and activities are anti-social. The credit card companies then deny them access to credit cards. That means these people and companies can't have a business or purchase anything themselves on credit. The goal is to starve those wicked people and organizations into compliance with the POP party's enlightened programs."

Bertram looked concerned. I could tell he was worried about his ability to order doggie treats off the TV. "Can I see the list?" he asked.

"Sure!" Libby volunteered. "Here it is."

Bertram sauntered over and read through the list. "Wait a minute!" he said in a panic. "The National Association of Dogs and the Denominational Order of God are on this list. I better tell Butch and Wolf right away!"

"Those two deplorable Dobermans are exactly the reason why your organizations were targeted," I retorted.

"And you are going to get the banks to go along with this, too?" Bertram asked in a hushed, horrified tone.

"Of course," I answered. "We want to bring the maximum amount of pressure on everyone who disagrees with us. If they starve or have to live in cardboard boxes, so much the better."

"Isn't this against the law?" Bertram asked, clearly grasping at straws.

"Nope," Libby responded. "It is against the law to discriminate against anyone based on race, ethnicity, and sexual orientation, but it is perfectly legal to discriminate against anyone based on their political beliefs."

"That's the beauty of financial blacklisting," I added "We don't have to rely on the legislature or courts to punish those who oppose us. We can do it ourselves!"

Just then the doorbell rang again. As I opened the door to greet the rest of the POP party Executive Board, Bertram dashed outside and down the street with a look of terror in his eyes. I smiled secretly to myself. "That worked better than the guillotine," I muttered to myself.

[17]

Bertram Interviews George Orwell

THE TWO DEPLORABLE Dobermans, Butch and Wolf, decided to combat the spread of financial blacklisting by starting a radio station to expound on and popularize their beliefs. They used their show dog earnings to start Canine Public Radio, call letters CPR. Bertram won the coveted morning slot. His first guest was the famous British author, George Orwell.

"Good morning CPR land! This is your host, Bertram, and welcome to *Breakfast with Bertram*. My guest this morning is the famed author of *Animal Farm*, Mr. George Orwell. Welcome!"

"Actually, George Orwell is my nom de plume."

"Huh? Nome what?" asked Bertram.

"Nom de plume. It's French for pen name. My real name is Eric Blair."

"Oh. I thought you were British," Bertram muttered. "Butch didn't say anything about that in the program notes."

Then speaking more audibly, Bertram asked, "Should I call you Eric or George?"

"Let's stick with George, shall we. It will cause less confusion."

SOCIALISM: IT'S A DOG'S LIFE

"George, I asked you here to discuss your very popular mini novel, *Animal Farm*. As you can imagine, any story about animals is very interesting to our listeners."

"Yes, I can well imagine," George responded. "I consider it one of my best works of fiction."

"And we at Canine Public Radio consider it one of the most stirring indictments of socialism ever written."

"It isn't meant as an indictment of socialism. You see, I am a devout democratic socialist," George casually stated. "The story is an indictment of the totalitarian fiends who misused socialism during my lifetime. People like Stalin and Mao. I believe that socialism under enlightened leadership will result in a utopian society."

Bertram scowled. He hadn't expected this. "So you don't agree that socialism will invariably result in a totalitarian society?" Bertram asked.

"Not at all. I don't see how that is possible," George responded.

Bertram continued probing. "Isn't it a basic tenet of socialism that everyone should receive things according to their needs and contribute according to their ability? That everyone should have the same?"

"Well, that is promoted more under communism, but socialism is not too far from that. Under socialism, all means of production should be held in common—by the government—to ensure an equitable distribution of wealth," George corrected. "Further, democratic socialists believe that decisions on matters of public concern, such as distribution of wealth, should be decided democratically, not by totalitarian despots."

"But, if everyone is rewarded based on how the public votes instead of how much they produce, won't people tend to vote themselves a generous share of the productive members' output, and won't that lead to the best producers ultimately reducing their output because there is no reward for working hard? Doesn't that lead to a rush to mediocrity at the expense of exceptionalism, thereby impoverishing the entire country?" Bertram expounded, drawing heavily from Butch's program notes.

"People have made that case," George allowed. "However, we democratic socialists believe that people are altruistic and, with the proper education, will gladly share what they produce without regard to who has produced the most or the least. In fact we believe that people will be motivated by a sense of pride in their ability to provide for others. We democratic socialists have great faith in our fellow man."

Bertram grimaced. His memory of the motivation he received in the POP party's re-education camp was not a happy one. "What if education doesn't work?" Bertram persisted.

"For those recalcitrant few, more disciplinary based measures may be needed."

"So you will punish those who don't work hard to produce at the rate the other voters think they should."

"That is a rather reactionary way of putting it, but yes, that is what will occur."

"And doesn't the need to punish those people inevitably lead to a totalitarian society like the one the pigs were running in your book?" Bertram was on a roll.

"You and I shall never agree on this, little dog," George answered condescendingly. "You see, your argument comes from what men are, mine from what men may become."

"So my position is based on reality and yours is based on hope?" countered Bertram.

"Precisely!"

SOCIALISM: IT'S A DOG'S LIFE

[18]

Bertram Learns a Really Big Word

I HAD JUST FINISHED listening to Bertram's interview of George Orwell on CPR radio and I was furious. I was muttering all the cutting remarks I would level at that little dog when he walked in the front door. And then he did.

"Hi!" Bertram greeted in a happy tone.

"I want to talk to you about that travesty of an interview you just conducted," I said sternly.

"Yeah, wasn't it great?" responded Bertram.

"No it wasn't! It was littered with misrepresentations." I couldn't contain my snarkiness.

"Like what?" asked Bertram.

"For example, George Orwell has been dead for many years. You obviously had an actor playing him."

"Ha! That's where you're wrong," Bertram cried out triumphantly. "It wasn't an actor at all. It was Wolf!"

"Well then, my hat's off to Wolf. He did a magnificent job defeating your juvenile arguments."

"Ha! Wrong again," Bertram announced. "We took a call-in poll after the show, and 38 dogs thought I won. There were only two votes for Wolf, and we suspect those were cat trolls, or maybe hyenas. There was a lot of laughing in the background."

"Remember our discussions about statistics? 40 is not a statistically relevant sample size. But I have to come back to the fact that your arguments were facile."

"Did you mean to say factual?" asked Bertram.

"No, I meant facile. It means . . . oh never mind. It is way over your head."

"So we're back to the short jokes again. You socialists always resort to name calling when you are losing an argument."

"I am not losing this argument. I am winning; you just don't know it yet. Your premise that socialist governments always result in totalitarianism is absurd."

"Okay," Bertram allowed, "name one socialist government that hasn't resulted in totalitarianism."

"Well that's easy," I began. "Let's see there was, no . . . what about, no not that one either . . . okay, yeah that, no . . . "

"Can't name one, can you. Checkmate!"

"Just because no one has done it yet doesn't mean it can't be done. I am positive that under the enlightened leadership of the POP party we will be the first to achieve a sustainable democratic utopian socialist society," I rebutted.

"Still clinging to that hope thing?" Bertram asked snidely.

"Well, I would rather sacrifice my country on the altar of hope than follow a dream squashing realist like you!" I replied angrily.

"That's not true. I have dreams. I do. I dream of a world where people are free to express their opinions without fear of punishment, where creatures are free to read the bible of their choice, where people are free from government intrusion, where everyone is free to keep what they earn, where lemonade is free from sugar taxes, where dogs are free to

BERTRAM LEARNS A REALLY BIG WORD

chase cats. I dream of a free society! FREEDOM!!!" exclaimed Bertram.

I suppressed a giggle. I was imaging him in a kilt with his face painted blue. "William Wallace you are not," I said gleefully; then continued, "but from your rant it sounds to me like you support a meritocracy."

"I'm not sure," Bertram waffled, "that's a lot of syllables."

"Let me explain it to you. A meritocracy is a system where people are promoted and compensated based on their ability and achievements," I explained.

Bertram's face brightened. "Oh, I see. I was a little confused there for a minute. I thought you were talking about mediocrity. But that merit thing, I like it."

"But don't you see," I chided, "a meritocracy is so unfair. People with the most abilities will get most of the money, and those with the least abilities will get the least. The government would have to step in to ensure an equitable distribution of wealth."

"Equitable by whose standards?" Bertram snarled.

"By the standards of the socialist electorate, if that isn't too big a word for you." I retorted, reverting to my former snarkiness.

"Yeah? Well . . . I have a big word for you!" Bertram barked.

"Fine. Let's hear it."

"I can't say it here. This is a children's story."

(Editor's note: Dear reader, it appears that even a little dog has more class than Congresswoman Tlaib.)

SOCIALISM: IT'S A DOG'S LIFE

[19]

Bertram and Ayn Rand's Ghost

"Good morning CPR land, and welcome to *Breakfast with Bertram*. Our guest today is the renowned author Ayn Rand. She is here to discuss her greatest work, that tribute to the productive, *Atlas Shrugged*. In the interest of full disclosure and not getting my tail slammed in the door when I get home, Ms. Rand has been dead for a while. Here to speak on her behalf is my associate, Wolf," Bertram explained.

"Before we start the interview, I would like to give our listeners a little background on the book," Bertram said, reading Butch's program notes verbatim. "The book is set in a time when socialist governments around the world, through their corrupt and ill advised socialist policies, have caused the collapse of the world economy, leaving their citizens destitute and desperate. America is the last remaining industrial powerhouse, but even here the socialist mindset is triumphing, even among most of the business leaders. Profit is thought immoral and competition wasteful. The sole purpose of business is held to be to 'provide for the common good.' Ever increasing government interference has created a landscape where business success is defined as having more and more influence

SOCIALISM: IT'S A DOG'S LIFE

with Washington politicians rather than positive growth based on innovation and efficiency. The result is declining production and declining employment. The story unfolds through the eyes of a young and dazzlingly competent business executive Dagny Taggart, as she struggles to keep her family's railroad alive despite declining employee competency, poorer customers, and unreliable suppliers. The national condition is worsened by the mysterious disappearances of the few remaining exceptional industrialists, technicians, workers, and artists. Will anyone come forward to save America, and thus the world? You'll have to read the book to find out.

"Good morning Ms. Rand and welcome to our show."

"Good morning. I am happy to be here," Wolf said in his best impression of a female voice as he assumed the role of Ayn Rand.

"I understand that you were born in Russia and immigrated to the United States after the Bolshevik revolution," Bertram said, consulting Butch's program notes.

"That is correct. Am I safe in assuming that you have read my book?" Wolf trilled.

"Well, I read the summary. The book was really long, over a thousand pages."

"Only a thousand pages? You must have the small print version. If you have studied my philosophy you will know that I believe that only things that are accomplished with hard work and determination are worthwhile," Wolf haughtily chastised the host as he took on the persona of Ayn Rand. "But you are only a little dog, and perhaps that was all you were capable of."

Bertram shot Wolf a dirty look. "Well that's very charitable of you," Bertram responded with a touch of sarcasm.

"Really, Mr. Russell. If you had read my book you would

SOCIALISM: IT'S A DOG'S LIFE

know that I consider charity born of pity to be immoral. It enslaves both the receiver and the giver," continued Wolf in a haughty voice.

"Wolf, cut it out!" Bertram whispered, leaning forward and covering his microphone. "You will upset the listeners. And knock off that fake accent."

Wolf had a look of panic in his eyes. "I can't help it," he whispered back. "It's like I've channeled her and now she is in control."

"Well Dobermans are Russian. Tell her to stop!" Bertram hissed.

"Dobermans are not Russian, they're German!" Wolf hissed back, now completely under the control of Ayn Rand.

Butch was in the control room waving his arms wildly at no one in particular. He looked like he was fighting off a swarm of hornets.

"What's the difference?" Bertram inquired in a hushed tone.

"Germans say 'Ja' and the Russians say 'Da.'"

"Well, tell her no da, no da!" Bertram commanded.

Butch continued gesticulating wildly in the control booth.

"Mr. Russell, may we continue the interview?" asked a calm and authoritative voice. Wolf's paws flew up to his mouth. His eyes were the size of silver dollars. He tried to say, 'It's not me! It's not me!' but the words didn't come out.

From up near the ceiling, the voice then asked again, "May we?" This time the request was more of a command than a question.

Butch had given up and was slumped silently over the control panel, and Wolf was huddled in a quivering mass on his chair, glassy eyed and foaming at the mouth.

"Okay," Bertram responded timidly. "Could you explain how your philosophy shaped the book?"

"With pleasure, Mr. Russell. You see, the real heroes in this world are those who use their minds and their drive to produce wealth. They worship life. They live by reason. These are the men of the mind. The villains are those who attempt to control and enslave the productive with guilt; guilt for their achievements and guilt for the wealth they have produced. These villains are the looters. Their goal is to rob the producers of their achievements and to consume what they themselves had no hand in producing. They worship death. They live by mysticism. The ultimate outcome of their policies is the total destruction of producers and wealth. In the beginning they rely on the greed of the voters, in the end, on their own totalitarianism."

"Sort of like the goose and the golden egg?" Bertram offered helpfully out of the *D.O.G.* bible parables. He was hoping to lighten up the tone a little.

"No, Mr. Russell," the voice intoned, "not like the goose and the golden egg. That fable is immoral. It implies that it is acceptable to rob the goose of its egg as long as one does not harm the goose."

Bertram glanced furtively over to Butch for support, but he was still slumped over his control panel in a near comatose condition.

"Let's talk about your book," Bertram said. "The hero, John Galt; who is John Galt?"

"That is the phrase of lost hope, of resignation, spoken by the shattered characters throughout the story."

"What phrase?"

"Who is John Galt?"

"That was what I just asked," Bertram repeated.

"Oh you little dog of limited comprehension . . . ," started the voice.

SOCIALISM: IT'S A DOG'S LIFE

BERTRAM AND AYN RAND'S GHOST

"Well, would you look at that, time's up. Good bye and thanks!" Bertam said quickly with an immense sigh of relief. Butch started to stir in the control booth. He cued the show theme music.

Wolf's eyes began to focus. "What the heck was that?" he asked, still a little stunned.

"I'm not sure, but I'm really glad it's over," Bertram replied.

A faint and ghostly voice came over the public address system saying, "Who is John Galt?"

As fast as they could, the three dogs high-tailed it out of the radio studio.

(Editor's note: Dear reader, this is a spoiler alert. Read no further if you intend to tackle Atlas Shrugged. For everyone else, John Galt is the hero. He defeats the looters who almost succeeded in destroying every economy in the world. The book is over 1,000 pages, but it's a great book and I recommend it.)

·· [20] ··

Bertram Finds Utopia

I WAS WAITING FOR Bertram when he came back to the house badly shaken by his interview with Ayn Rand. He went directly to his favorite perch on the back of the couch and curled up into a tight, trembling little ball.

"What a great show!" I congratulated him. "It was a mesmerizing piece of drama. Whoever wrote that script should get an award."

"It wasn't a script, it was a real ghost," Bertram answered meekly, his nose still tucked firmly under his tail. "But it is all taken care of now. Butch and Wolf put on their deacon robes and conducted a full blown exorcism of the studio. Holy water from a Saint Bernard's water bowl, Pig Latin incantations, the whole shebang. It was a phantom flush." Bertram relaxed a little and started coming out of his shell.

"There are no such things as ghosts," I remarked. "But since you have exhibited such talent, I wanted to float an idea pass you for your show. I was at one of the POP party's guest lecturer series recently and heard an extremely fascinating talk by Professor Nowitt Awl from Y.U. University on Thomas More's book *Utopia*. I think it would be a great topic

BERTRAM FINDS UTOPIA

for your show and it would definitely add balance to CPR's programming."

"This More guy, is he dead or alive?" Bertram asked cautiously.

"He's been dead for several hundred years."

"We aren't doing any more interviews with dead authors. Not after today. Not even after the exorcism," Bertram said forcefully.

"I'm not suggesting you interview More," I elaborated. "I'm suggesting that you interview Nowitt. He is on the POP party's Education Subcommittee. I'm sure I can get him to agree."

"Are all professors at Y.U. members of the POOP party?"

"POP party. And yes they are. We wouldn't have it any other way."

"Okay, we'll consider it." Bertram was feeling a little safer and sat up. "But you have to give me some background on the book first."

"Well, the book is a description of More's thoughts on what a perfect society would look like. It is one of the few English books that the Soviets allowed to be printed in Russia."

"You mean that the Union of Soviet Socialist Republics banned books? Isn't that a violation of free speech? Didn't the NAZI's do the same thing? Butch told me that NAZI in German stands for National Socialism," Bertram said excitedly.

I ignored those gratuitous comments and continued, "More called his make believe country 'Utopia' because it is Greek for 'no place'. That is how the word entered the English language. The story is set in the new world."

"No place is the perfect name for a place that is impossible to exist," Bertram noted.

Not to be outdone by a little dog, I pressed on. "More posited a socialist society where everything was held in

SOCIALISM: IT'S A DOG'S LIFE

common by the people, down to their houses and pots and pans. Since everything was held in common, there was no money. People went to warehouses around the country and took out what they needed. They restocked the warehouses from their work products. Everyone was required to work six hours a day at their assigned activity. The rest of their waking hours were to be spent in study or working a skilled trade. Idle time was not tolerated."

"I'm not sure what 'posited' means, but it sounds socialist," Bertram said."

(Editor's note: Dear reader, it was brought to my attention that Bertram may not be the only one confused by the word 'posited'. In this context it means to offer a thought or theory. Looks like I'll have to have yet another discussion with the elitist author about showing off his vocabulary.)

"Anyway, what happened if someone didn't obey the work rules? And did everyone have to work?" continued Bertram.

"That seldom happened because everyone was thoroughly indoctrinated into the importance of supporting the common good over individual wants. But if someone did break the work rules, they were punished. And yes, everyone had to work, except for government officials and priests," I explained.

"How were they punished?" Bertram persisted. "And exempting government officials sounds like your brand of socialism!"

"Lazy people were made slaves of the state," I responded.

"So you're a part-time slave when you're good and a full-time slave when you're bad? Sounds like Mao's China. Did everyone have to wear the same Mao jackets?" Bertram chuckled. He was laying the sarcasm on a little thick.

"Yes, everyone wore the same grey clothes to show modesty and to prevent the appearance of differences in wealth or status. But that's not the point. Utopia wasn't a real place; it was just a thought experiment. The interesting thing is that even as far back as five hundred years ago people were thinking about socialism as a preferred form of government. I really think your CPR listeners would enjoy hearing Professor Awl's lecture on More's book.

"Yeah, no thanks. It's been over five hundred years and not one success yet," Bertram decided. "We'll go with John Locke instead."

(Editor's note again: Dear reader, John Locke was a famous English philosopher from the Enlightenment. His writings had a huge influence on our founding fathers' views on liberty. These views were incorporated into the Declaration of Independence.)

"You know that he is also dead," I pointed out.

"Hmmm. Everyone we want to interview turns up dead," Bertram mused. "Coincidence? I think not!"

·· [21] ··

Bertram and Diversity

I WAS PRACTICING MY speech for my run for Chairman of the POP party's Subcommittee on Destruction of Political Dissent in front of Bertram. There was a five minute time limit, and no rebuttals or questions allowed. I was running against Professor Nowitt Awl, so I wanted to be well prepared. As a university professor, Nowitt had the luxury of unlimited paid preparation time and a host of grad students to help him write his speech.

"... and the discord and disharmony that accompanies the political messages of the opposing parties divides us, disunites us, and fills our citizenry with wrong-headed notions. We must pluck these weeds now, before they can sow the seeds of further hate and discontent in our beautiful socialist garden. Diversity is our greatest strength. Therefore, we must support the righteous struggles of our brothers and sisters of different ethnicities, different races, different sexual orientations..."

"I have a question," interrupted Bertram.

"Bertram, don't interrupt, I'm timing this! But since you've already ruined this practice run, what's your question?"

"Well," Bertram began, "you are railing against diversity in one instance, and then you start praising it in the next. What gives?"

"You missed my point. Diversity in political thought is dangerous and is not to be tolerated. Diversity of people is a beautiful thing that is to be celebrated."

"Even Bubbas?" asked Bertram.

"This was covered in your POP party re-education class. Bubbas are not people, but are a dangerous group of anti-socialist political radicals who are supercharged on a noxious blend of toxic masculinity and white privilege. They must be ridiculed and denounced. Do you understand?"

"Maybe," Bertram replied. "This kind of reminds me of last night's N.A.D. meeting."

I didn't see how anything about N.A.D. could relate to our discussion. "I don't see how anything about N.A.D. can relate to our discussion," I stated flatly.

"Well," Bertram said, "we always start our meetings with a pledge to the organization. It goes like this: We, the proud and loyal membership, do hereby pledge to protect the Na . . . "

"Stop right there!" I commanded.

" . . . tional Association of Dogs from ridicule and dishonor," Bertram concluded. "Why do you want me to stop?"

"Never mind," I answered. "I don't see how your pledge relates to our discussion."

"It doesn't, but I was getting there. After the pledge one of the members will recite a speech from a dictator. We all make fun of it and laugh. If he can do it in a cat voice it is even funnier," Bertram explained. "Last night it was Joe's turn."

"Joe, the cocker spaniel from next door?" I interrupted.

"That's right, Joe Cocker," Bertram replied. "Anyway, he did a speech from Stalin about moving wheat out of the Ukraine

and sending it to the rest of the Soviet Union. He called it 'Uncle Joe, He'll Lift Us Up Where We Belong.' Joe does a killer cat voice. It was hilarious!"

(Editor's note: Dear reader, 'Uncle Joe' was the Allies' nick name for Joseph Stalin during World War II. And for the younger crowd, one of rock star Joe Cocker's biggest hits was 'Up Where We Belong.' My wife says jokes aren't funny if they have to be explained, but I think she's wrong.)

"Bertram!" I said in a shocked voice. "That's horrible. Stalin's speech was a very important speech about creating an artificial famine in the Ukraine to punish political opposition. As a result of the famine, millions of people who opposed Stalin died."

"Sort of like financial blacklisting?" Bertram offered, pretending to be helpful.

I didn't appreciate that parallel being drawn so starkly and scowled fiercely at Bertram. He smiled back benignly. He was getting far too good at hiding his thoughts.

"Anyway," Bertram continued, "I still don't understand why the POP party is so against other political opinions. Why not let the electorate decide? In Wolf's sermon last Sunday, he said that politics is the marketplace of ideas and the voters are the shoppers."

"And every marketplace must be tightly regulated by the government to protect the greater good. The so called 'marketplace of ideas' is no exception," I retorted.

"But don't you agree that having the most number of potential solutions gives us the greatest opportunity to develop successful policies?" Bertram persisted.

"No I don't. The only policies that will lead to a utopian

society are progressive socialist ones. Any other options just create confusion and disunity among the average people, thereby delaying our wonderful utopia and will not be allowed. Any competing ideas must be suppressed immediately."

"Yeah, that came through pretty clearly in your speech," Bertram stated.

"Did it really? Thanks!" I said gratefully.

"Good luck with your speech and enjoy your book burning!" Bertram responded as he switched on the new educational TV.

'Book burning?' I thought to myself. 'Whatever is he talking about?'

SOCIALISM: IT'S A DOG'S LIFE

[22]

Bertram and Individual Rights

Libby Real, Professor Nowitt Awl, and I were having an impromptu gathering at my house to discuss how best to achieve our goals of a socialist utopia. Bertram was stretched out on a chair facing the window with his belly to the sun. He was doing his best impression of a solar collector.

Libby said, "We don't seem to be moving fast enough towards our objective. I wonder why?"

"Perhaps we are trying to accomplish too much too fast," I opined.

"Yes, I think you have a point there," Nowitt acknowledged. "The common citizen lacks the time and the aptitude to really appreciate what we are doing for him. It is too much for him to assimilate and the pressure of rapid change invariably generates its own inertia. I propose that an incremental approach may yield the best long term results."

"Hey!" Bertram yelled from across the room, "What language is the Prof speaking?"

"It's English," I yelled back. "And mind your own business."

"Nowitt, I believe you are correct," Libby stated. "We need to better schedule the implementation of our agenda.

SOCIALISM: IT'S A DOG'S LIFE

By moving forward with baby steps that include benefits the average citizen believes will be free to him, we should have less opposition."

"Sounds good to me!" I chimed in. "By the way Nowitt, congratulations on winning the chairmanship the other day."

We then proceeded to develop an implementation outline and schedule to present at the next meeting of the POP party Executive Board. When we finished, Libby and Nowitt took their leave and departed.

"What was that all about?" Bertram asked.

"Just a planning discussion for the POP party," I answered evasively.

"What's the grand old POOP party up to now?" he inquired.

"POP party. And we were strategizing how to tailor our activities to best accomplish our long term goals. A certain amount of obfuscation may be in order." I knew that 'obfuscation' would throw the little dog off the scent.

"Not sure what 'obfuscation' is, but it sounds Michael Evilian," Bertram replied.

"Michael Evilian?" I asked.

"Yeah, you know, it's named after that Italian guy that wrote the book on how to be a sneaky dictator," Bertram elaborated.

"Oh, you mean Machiavellian, and the book was called *The Prince*. Your description of the book's purpose lacks nuance," I said.

"New ants? I don't understand why you are suddenly in favor of new ants, especially after you put that ant poison in the kitchen cabinets," Bertram said, somewhat flabbergasted.

(Editor's note: Dear reader, I give up. Get a dictionary.)

SOCIALISM: IT'S A DOG'S LIFE

"Never mind," I responded. "But it would be helpful if I could better understand the common man's objections to socialism. Perhaps you can tell me why you resist so fervently?"

"Individual rights," Bertram said flatly and with authority.

"Like what?" I asked.

"Well, let's start with freedom of speech. Socialists are against freedom of speech."

"No we're not," I defended. "We are just against speech that is against socialism, or that impugns protected groups."

"There you go again Mr. Socialist. Using big words like impugns," Bertram growled.

"Fine," I said, "give me another example."

"The right of people to keep the fruits of their labor."

"Bertram, we've had this discussion before. It is a matter of fairness. No one should have more than they need when others are in want. The excess 'fruits', as you put it, rightfully belong to the community."

"When you say that the fruits of my labor belong to someone else it sounds a lot like slavery. Like I am the slave to some anonymous person who has a right to my stuff," Bertram countered.

"Really Bertram! What an unenlightened and selfish attitude. With that sort of thinking, I am surprised that you didn't bring up the right to bear arms!" I retorted.

"You can wear whatever sleeve length you like," Bertram replied. "But I think that is a relatively minor individual freedom."

"Not bare arms, BEAR arms," I responded with appropriate emphasis.

"Sounds the same to me."

"Okay, let me put it in a way that will make it easier to

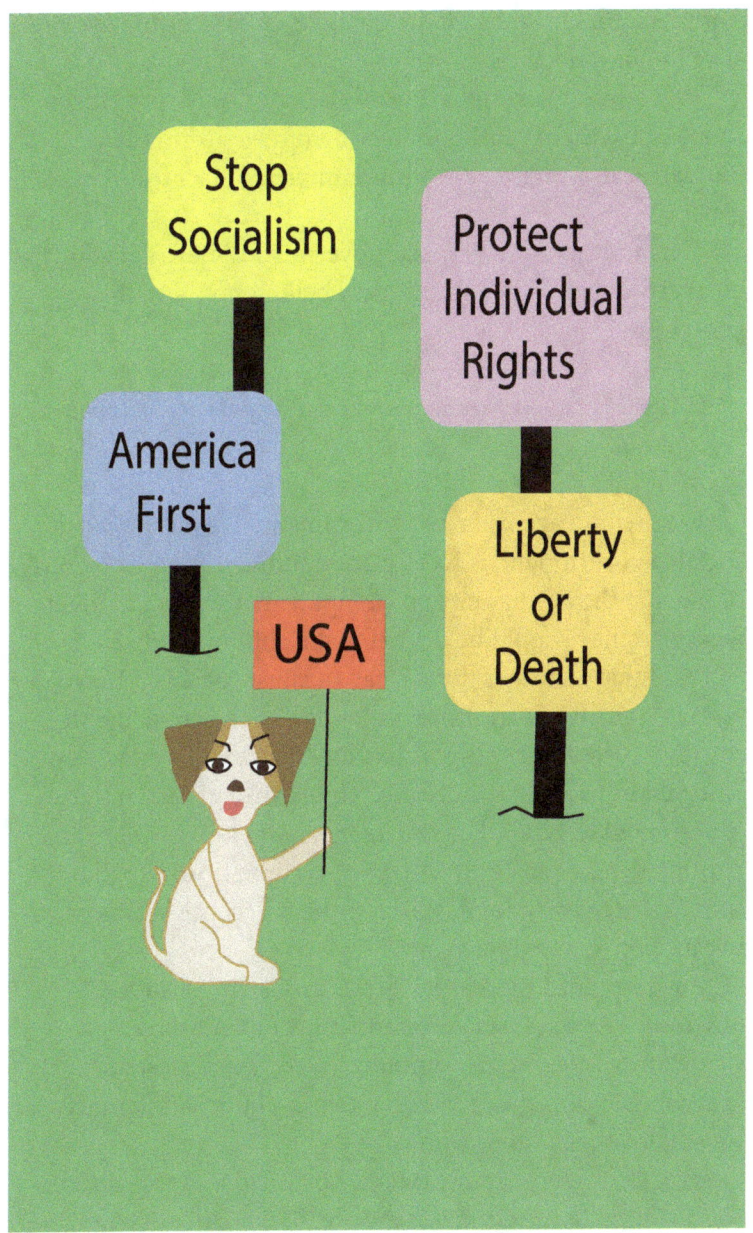

SOCIALISM: IT'S A DOG'S LIFE

comprehend. Do you support the right of citizens to have firearms?" I inquired.

"Of course!" Bertram said enthusiastically. "Every citizen should have the means to protect themselves from cat burglars, cat-a-pults, cat-a-tonic zombies, in fact from cats in general!

"Oh, and against a despotic government," Bertram added as an afterthought. "After all, a little rebellion now and then is a good thing!"

(Editor's note: Dear reader, my sincerest apologies to Thomas Jefferson.)

"A rebellion against a just government, like our planned socialist government, is NOT a good thing. It is now obvious to me that the average citizen cannot be trusted to use firearms wisely, so they should be denied that right," I pontificated.

"And that's another thing I have against socialist," Bertram railed. "You always treat the rest of us like children; like we can't be trusted to be responsible and take care of ourselves. And you guys act like individual rights are a gift from the government to be applied or denied as you see fit!" Bertram continued his rant. "Individual rights come from a higher source than government. We have them because WE exist, not because the government exists."

At this point I was exasperated. "Honestly, isn't there anything you and I can agree on, little dog?" I asked.

Bertram thought for a minute. "Well," he suggested, "perhaps we can agree that, despite our political differences, we still love each other, don't we?"

That stopped me in my tracks. I brushed aside a tear that was forming in the corner of my eye. "Yes we do, Bertram, yes

BERTRAM AND INDIVIDUAL RIGHTS

we do," I said gently as I bent down to scratch him behind his ears.

Bertram smiled up at me and wagged his tail happily.

The End

www.ingramcontent.com/pod-product-compliance
Lightning Source LLC
Chambersburg PA
CBHW071005080526
44587CB00015B/2352